THE
CAMBRIDGE
STORY THE IMPACT OF CHRISTIANITY IN ENGLAND

LIVING HISTORY
EXHIBITION AT THE
ROUND CHURCH

THE CAMBRIDGE STORY

AN INTRODUCTION

This booklet is a reproduction of the Exhibition in the Round Church, Cambridge. It aims to tell the Cambridge Story from the Romans to the 20th Century. For each historical period, it contains the national and cultural **CONTEXT** with a particular emphasis on the influence of Christianity on our culture. There is then some more detailed **COMMENT** and, finally, a local picture of **CAMBRIDGE**.

We believe it is not possible to understand our society without reference to its Christian foundations. The contribution of Christianity to the development of education and the growth of modern science, to our ideas of religious and political freedom and to our notions of human rights cannot be overlooked and can all be illustrated in Cambridge. Not that Christianity was ever perfectly applied, as the Crusades, slavery and social injustice in our history all show. However, Christianity provided the framework for abuses to be criticised and progress to be made.

ABOUT THE AUTHOR

IAN COOPER was educated at Monkton Combe School, Bath, read history at Jesus College, Cambridge, taught at St Clement Danes Grammar School, London, and worked at L'Abri Fellowship, a Christian study centre in Hampshire, England. He now works as Senior Tutor for Christian Heritage, Cambridge. He is particularly interested in how cultures are shaped by their ideas.

CONTENTS

1 THE ROMANS
1st-5th Century

CONTEXT

The road you have come in on is an old Roman road – the Via Devana. The Roman army had an encampment just across the river on Castle Hill. This was a frontier area between the Celtic tribes of the Trinovantes and the Catuvellauni, so the Romans were here nearly 2,000 years ago. What many don't realise is that Christianity has also been in Britain since the time of the Romans. It was sufficiently widespread for the churches in Britain to send bishops to the Synod of Arles in the south of France as early as AD 312. This is not surprising as Britain, or Britannia, was not just a remote outpost of the Roman Empire but a valued province, with extensive trade links through which the Christian faith first came. Also, Constantine the Great, who first tolerated Christianity with his Edict of Milan in AD 313, became Emperor in York. This would have given the churches in Britain a certain credibility.

COMMENT

The extent of Christianity in England in Roman times is not fully appreciated since under the onslaught of the pagan Saxons in the 5th Century the faith declined and virtually disappeared. No written records or intact buildings from the Roman era were left. However, today we no longer have to rely on a few stories, like that of St Alban, recorded by chroniclers such as Bede, as archaeology is helping us to fill in the gaps. Artefacts with Christian symbols such as the Alpha and Omega and Chi-Rho have been found in many parts of the country. Further, it is increasingly clear that many later Christian sites used earlier ones from the Roman period, as at Canterbury. A particularly fascinating piece of evidence from the late 4th Century for the prevalence of Christianity is a curse directed at a thief inscribed on a piece of lead and thrown into the sacred spring of Sulis Minerva in Bath. The curse starts 'Whether pagan or Christian…' presupposing a society where both commonly coexisted.

ST ALBAN, THE FIRST MARTYR IN ENGLAND, CIRCA AD 251-253

Alban was a Romano-British soldier stationed at Verulamium – modern St Albans. He gave shelter to a Christian priest and was so struck by his character that he was converted. Becoming a Christian was then a capital offence and when he was discovered he was executed and thus became the first Christian martyr in Britain.

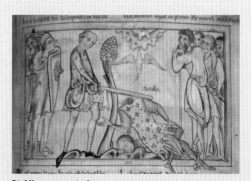

St Alban executed

CAMBRIDGE

The most important legacy from the Roman period is the site of the road through Cambridge running from the modern Hills Road to Castle Street across the river. This used to be the Via Devana, a military road linking the fortress towns of Colchester and Leicester via Godmanchester. The Roman settlement was near Castle Mound, where excavations have shown a large site with a fort. This was probably erected after the great Iceni revolt led by Queen Boudicca in AD 60-61, which started in nearby Norfolk. To the north of Cambridge, the Romans started the drainage of the fens, for example, at Car Dyke.

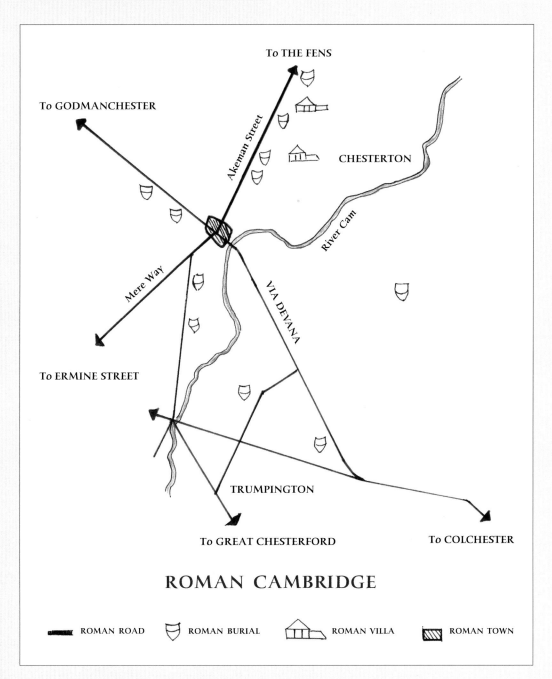

To THE FENS

To GODMANCHESTER

Akeman Street

CHESTERTON

River Cam

Mere Way

VIA DEVANA

To ERMINE STREET

TRUMPINGTON

To GREAT CHESTERFORD

To COLCHESTER

ROMAN CAMBRIDGE

ROMAN ROAD   ROMAN BURIAL   ROMAN VILLA   ROMAN TOWN

2 THE SAXONS
5th-11th Century

CONTEXT

With the collapse of the Roman Empire in the early 5th Century, fierce raiders came across the North Sea: the Angles, Saxons and Jutes. They began to settle on the east coast and then pushed their way into what they eventually made England – 'the land of the Angles'. Christianity survived with the Romano-British Celts in Cornwall and Wales in the West, who passed their faith on to the Irish through St Patrick, but elsewhere the country reverted to paganism. The newcomers worshipped Tiw, the sky god, Woden, the god of wisdom and war, Thor, the protector of farmers and Freya, the goddess of fertility, from which we get our weekdays, Tuesday, Wednesday, Thursday and Friday.

Icelandic 10th Century. Image of Thor

The conversion of these 'heathen' came about in the north through the efforts of Celtic missionaries like St Aidan of Lindisfarne and in the South through Roman missionaries like St Augustine, who came to Kent in AD 597. The Celtic monks were the fruit of St Patrick's work in Ireland and then of St Columba in Scotland. Columba's monastery at Iona sent St Aidan whilst Augustine was sent by Pope Gregory the Great. These two different traditions were united in favour of the Roman one at the Council of Whitby in AD 664. Gradually Christianised, Anglo-Saxon England saw something of a cultural flowering. The Venerable Bede in his monastery at Jarrow wrote his *Ecclesiastical History of the English People*. The great scholar Alcuin of York was

Alfred the Great

called to teach at the court of Charlemagne in the 8th Century. In the 9th Century, Alfred the Great of Wessex and his successors united the Anglo-Saxon kingdoms and absorbed further waves of Danish raiders and settlers and so created a united England.

Saxon costume

COMMENT

MONASTICISM

When Christianity became official in the Roman Empire it lost some of its integrity. Some Christians tried to maintain the pure ideals of the early Church by adopting vows of poverty, chastity and obedience and separating themselves from the world in monasteries. St Benedict, with his Rule at Monte Cassino, helped to shape this monastic ideal. While this kind of ascetic spirituality could not be justified from the Bible and owed much to Greek thought, it was these dedicated monks who converted Europe and maintained learning and faith through times of extreme turbulence and turmoil.

CONVERSION OF EUROPE

Explaining why the pagan tribes of Europe eventually became Christian, to form Christendom, is partly a matter of understanding that Christianity was seen to confer cultural advantage. Pagan rulers, like Ethelbert in Kent and Clovis in France, saw that Christianising their kingdoms gave them access to educated officials and a certain prestige. Of course, the hope and love of the Christian gospel exhibited in the lives of men like St Patrick, St Columba and St Aidan is also crucial. It is true that much superstition and violence remained, but the new faith began to tame and civilise some of the barbaric practices of these tribesmen.

CAMBRIDGE

Cambridge or, as the Anglo-Saxon Chronicle of AD 875 calls it, Grantebrycge was a frontier town between the Mercians and Angles and then later part of the Danelaw (Danish territory). Because of this, it saw its fair share of action, including being burnt to the ground in 1010 by Danish raiders. However, it was sufficiently important to have a Mint, and the Saxon stone tower of St Bene't's, built about 1025, still stands. Christianity came to the region in the 7th Century through St Fursey and St Felix from Burgundy and was encouraged by, amongst others, the Saxon princess Etheldreda who founded the Abbey of Ely.

St Bene't's tower

Lindisfarne

3 THE NORMANS
11th-12th Century

CONTEXT

Anglo-Saxon England came to an end in 1066 with the Conquest by William the Bastard, Duke of Normandy. Thereafter, there was a new ruling elite who were to speak Norman French for the next 300 years until the Hundred Years War, when English was adopted. The presence of this alien occupying elite perhaps helps to explain the origin of the English class system.

The French connection was also to be expanded by the next dynasty, the Plantagenets, who involved England in endless and fruitless wars in France. However, the Normans brought a new energy and sophistication to running the country that saw a great period of abbey, cathedral and castle building, though, remember, with Saxon-forced labour. Locally, the cathedrals of Ely, Peterborough and Norwich were all started at this time. The Normans were also a channel for the Church reform movement associated with Pope Gregory VII. This was to reinvigorate the Church through men like the new

Ely Cathedral

Norman Archbishop of Canterbury, Lanfranc. And it is wrong, perhaps, to idealise Anglo-Saxon England as it is estimated that 10 per cent of the population were thralls – that is, slaves – something that Lanfranc's successor, Anselm, sought to end.

William II of England appoints St Anselm Archbishop of Canterbury

COMMENT

THE CRUSADES

From the end of the 11th Century to the late 13th Century the knights of Christendom went on Crusade. Encouraged by popes offering immunity from purgatory, they sought to drive out the Muslims from the Holy Land and safeguard Jerusalem for Christian pilgrims. That their wrong-headed idealism soon degenerated into massacre, intrigue and land-grabbing, thus betraying the peaceful credentials of the Gospel, took a long time to register. It is true of course that it was no more than the other side of the coin to Islam's imperial jihad or holy war, but that can be no excuse. The Crusades are just an instance of a cultural Christianity which was not truly Christian.

CAMBRIDGE

The hated Sheriff Picot represented the new kind of oppressive Norman overlord in Cambridge. Within a couple of years of the Conquest, 27 houses were knocked down to make way for the great wooden motte and bailey fortress on Castle Hill. This was built as a base for the campaign against Hereward the Wake, the Saxon resistance fighter in the Fens. Sadly, he was to be betrayed by the monks of Ely. Later, Edward I was to rebuild the castle in stone. Norman rule did, however, mean security, and the town prospered because of it. In 1086, the Domesday Book recorded 400 burgesses in Cambridge and Sheriff Picot,

Castle Mound today

perhaps seeking to make amends, founded a monastery at Barnwell.

Motte and bailey

Norman Architecture, The Round Church, Cambridge

4 THE MIDDLE AGES
12th-15th Century

CONTEXT

This was the time of knights and peasants, tournaments and fairs, new towns and merchant guilds, roads no more than tracks travelled by pack horse and pilgrims and over all, soaring heavenwards, the great Gothic cathedrals. Feudalism held it all together. It was a system where, at the top, the king gave land to his barons in return for military service and at the

Leper Chapel, Cambridge

bottom the local lord of the manor gave strips of land to the peasants in return for their working on his land. Parallel to this political/military hierarchy and legitimising it was the ecclesiastical hierarchy of archbishops, bishops and priests as well as abbots and monks, all of whom looked to the Pope in Rome for guidance and authority. Cambridge was under the feudal magnate the Lord Bishop of Ely and is still in that diocese today. In this context the pressure was for a merely cultural Christianity conformed to this world's standards. However, within these constraints, the Church promoted education, for example, the Bishop of Ely founded the first Cambridge college, Peterhouse, in 1284 and cared for the poor and sick. St John's College was originally a hospital, and outside the town is the chapel of St Mary Magdalene, originally the chapel to a leper hospital. Also, attempts were made to regulate economic life with the practice of the 'just price' and the ban on usury.

COMMENT

FEUDALISM

Feudalism was a system geared for war. It aimed at providing for the hugely expensive armoured cavalry deemed essential for external security and internal peace. However, despite the ideals of chivalry, it was a warlord culture that exploited the mass of peasants and provoked civil wars like the Wars of the Roses. When not causing chaos at home, the knights were causing mayhem abroad, in Wales, Ireland, Scotland or France. The absence of further invasion of England is argued in defence of the system, but surely it could have been different: a rural society without feudalism where everyone had a small farm protected by a citizen army – a farmers' republic.

Suppression of Lollards

THE LOLLARDS

As the Church was integrated into the established order, it meant that there were always those who tried to capture its original ideals, like St Francis in Italy or the Poor Men of Lyons in France. In England, one such group was the Lollards, which may mean 'mutterers' or 'mumblers'. They were influenced by the brilliant Oxford scholar John Wycliffe, who was deeply critical of the power and wealth of the church and who translated the

John Wycliffe preaching

Bible into English from the standard Latin Vulgate. He wanted Christians to be able to understand God's truth directly for themselves. He is sometimes called the Morning Star of the Reformation and was to be a great influence on John Hus of Bohemia (Czech Republic). The Lollards were ruthlessly suppressed as heretics, especially when their ideals were associated with political unrest, such as in the great Peasants' Revolt of 1381.

CAMBRIDGE

Navigable from the sea, protected by a castle, at a good bridging point and in the heart of a rich agricultural region, Cambridge was destined to prosper. In the early 13th Century this was helped by the patronage of King John. He gave the town a charter and the right to hold the Stourbridge Fair, which became one of the greatest trade fairs in Europe (and later would be the inspiration for John Bunyan's Vanity Fair in *Pilgrim's Progress*). Supported by this prosperity, religious houses like those of the Benedictines were established. These were centres of learning and they helped to attract the first students fleeing from 'town/gown' riots in Oxford in 1209. The masters and students of the new University at first rented rooms in the town in

which to live and study, but gradually these gave way to the more secure colleges like Peterhouse, 1284, Clare, 1326, Pembroke, 1347, Trinity Hall, 1350 and Corpus Christi, 1352. In 1318 the Pope recognised Cambridge as a Studium Generale, a centre for higher education. All

Corpus Christi Old Court

learning was in Latin and was designed to give at undergraduate level a proficiency in the language and its classic texts, along with mathematics. At the doctoral level, medicine, law and theology were studied. In those days, the University provided a chance for poor, bright boys to get onto the career ladder of the Church, which was the only avenue of advancement open to them. In Cambridge as well, town/gown quarrels were frequent but the University was usually supported by the King, as it was the source of his trained officials. In the Peasants' Revolt of 1381, the frustrated townsfolk burnt the University records and denounced university privileges. However, after the Bishop of Norwich sent troops to crush the revolt, the

Master and students

town was officially subordinated to the University, which was given various legal privileges, including the right to control the market, which remained until the mid 19th Century.

TOWN/GOWN QUARRELS WERE FREQUENT

5 THE NEW LEARNING
15th-16th Century

CONTEXT

The 15th Century saw what some have called the waning of the Middle Ages. The Church, with its worldly wealth and power, lost prestige. The papacy, in particular, became discredited after the Avignon Captivity, when it was under the control of the French kings. Feudal ties began to unravel with the rise of the money economy. Trade and towns became more important and in the country more peasants started working for wages. Printing with movable type was introduced by Gutenberg in Germany in 1453 and later by Caxton in England in 1476, creating a much larger reading public.

Printing press

This, along with the maritime explorations of men like Bartholomew Diaz, Christopher Columbus and Vasco Da Gama, started to open up new horizons. The cultural consensus began to be more open to change. In Italy, especially, there was a renewed interest in the writers of classical Greece and Rome and a mentality which identified itself as 'humanist' took root. These influences gradually spread to England and were associated with men like Sir Thomas More the Lord Chancellor, Dean Colet of St Paul's Cathedral, and John Fisher, Chancellor of Cambridge University.

COMMENT

It is interesting to note that, before the Reformation, so many realised the need for Church reform, chiefly through better education. This was not just in England, but throughout Europe – witness the great work of Cardinal Ximenes in Spain. Most, like Fisher, wanted no change to the basic teaching of the Church, just better teaching and better living. Few realised where the 'new learning' and the desire for Church reform might go. When Luther got angry over the sale of forgiveness and indulgences, he had no idea that he had started the Reformation. But the die was cast. Some, like Erasmus, were appalled and tried to remain above the fray. Others, like More, tried to stop the Reformation; More as Chancellor was a noted burner of heretics. Others, like William Tyndale, knew that the 'new learning' was to advance the Reformation. His ground-breaking New Testament, translated into English from the original Greek, was produced while on the run in the Low Countries, where, after betrayal, he was burnt.

CAMBRIDGE

In 1441, the pious Henry VI founded King's College and started building the magnificent King's College Chapel. The extent of his piety might be questioned, however, when it is borne in mind that a quarter of the town was destroyed, including houses, workshops and

King's College Chapel

churches, all for his grandiose project. It was hardly conducive to good town relations. It was also ironic that Cambridge was chosen by Henry VI for its being free from the taint of any Lollardry, given its future Reformation associations. However, his zeal for education was part of a movement that was pushing Cambridge into the cultural mainstream. Lady Margaret Beaufort, Henry's niece and mother of Henry VII, was similarly interested in

Erasmus

John Fisher and Lady Margaret Beaufort

education and Church reform. With the help of John Fisher, she founded both Christ's College in 1505 and St John's College in 1511. She also funded Erasmus's crucial stay in Cambridge, where he produced the Greek New Testament in 1516. Erasmus was the leading scholar in Europe and also a brilliant satirist. He savaged the failings of the Church, both in his Colloquies and in his *In Praise of Folly*. His Greek New Testament was part of his more serious scholarship. Up till then, the standard Bible had been the Latin Vulgate produced by Jerome in the 5th Century. Erasmus's Greek New Testament got closer to the original, sometimes with radical results. For instance, the Vulgate translates one passage as 'do penance', whereas the Greek is more accurately translated 'repent', indicating an attitude of the heart rather than a superficial ritual.

6 THE REFORMATION
16th Century

CONTEXT

During the 16th Century, England changed from a pious Catholic country to a defiantly Protestant one. It was to be the Anglican variety of Protestantism, complete with Cranmer's priceless *Book of Common Prayer* and the Authorised Version (King James Version) of the Bible in 1611. What it meant in practice was that the sermon took the place of the mass, while the minister, now often a married man, replaced the priest. The key teaching was that the Bible alone was the source of authority (sola scriptura) and that salvation was a product of faith rather than of human merit (sola fide).

Throughout this period, Cambridge was centrally involved. Luther's ideas were discussed by young intellectuals in the White Horse Inn, nicknamed 'Little Germany'. Many of those who took part in these discussions were to become leaders of the Reformation, like Hugh Latimer (Clare College), Nicholas Ridley (Pembroke College) and Thomas Cranmer (Jesus College). All three were burnt as heretics in Oxford under Queen Mary. This is a reminder that the Reformation came at great cost. The reaction against the persecution of 'Bloody Mary' in the 1550s, when about 300 died, was one factor that made England irrevocably Protestant. That it was a mod-

Site of the White Horse Inn
Known as 'Little Germany' where Cambridge scholars debated the works of Martin Luther in the early sixteenth century
A birthplace of the Reformation in England

erate, broad Protestantism – Anglicanism – was due to the skill of her successor, Queen Elizabeth, with her Act of Uniformity 1559.

COMMENT

In recent times, some historians have questioned the Reformation in England. They have doubted how far the medieval Church was in need of reform, downplayed the extent of popular support for the Reformation, emphasised the role of the monarchy in imposing the Reformation and have questioned the value of a defiant English Protestant identity, which was alleged to cause strife in Europe. Firstly, this ignores the contemporary criticisms of the Church, for example by Erasmus, who, when he wrote his *In Praise of Folly*, was actually staying with More. Secondly, though Henry VIII started the Reformation process because of his need for a divorce which the Pope had refused, the new faith took popular root. Even if unintended, Henry's allowing the Great Bible in 1540 into every parish was a crucial cause of this. Furthermore, the extent to which Protestantism took hold is the only explanation for the resistance to Mary's attempt to return England to Catholicism. It was largely ordinary people who were burnt in the fires of Smithfield in London. Thirdly, it overlooks that the defiant Protestantism which seemed to cause so much strife arose out of a defensive posture. It was the Catholic superpower of the time, Spain, that sent the Armada in 1588 and waged a war of terror against the Dutch Protestants. In France, the Massacre of St Bartholomew in 1572 had wiped out all the leading French Protestants (Huguenots). England feared the worst. Moreover, it is important to see the true achievement of the Reformation. The fact that a person could approach God directly and personally and experience forgiveness without the mediation of a priest and read God's Word for himself was wonderfully liberating. Also, the Reformation gave a new respect to marriage and the family and to secular vocations. Being spiritual was no longer a question of going to a monastery but of serving God at home and at work.

THE DISSOLUTION OF THE MONASTERIES AND THE LIBRARY AT CORPUS CHRISTI

Henry VIII dissolved the monasteries to get their vast estates and to break the power of the Church. The beautiful buildings were abandoned and the monks pensioned off. The vast wealth gained gave a great opportunity to have a school in every parish as in Scotland, yet it was mostly wasted on wars against France. Moreover, the welfare which the monasteries had provided had to be replaced by new Poor Laws. Amongst the great treasures of the monasteries were their books and manuscripts which were to have a Cambridge connection. They could all have been lost were it not for the zeal of Archbishop Matthew Parker who, in the early years of Elizabeth's reign, scoured the country to save the books and manuscripts and later deposited them in his old college, Corpus Christi. They included the Canterbury Gospels which were brought to England by St Augustine in 597. They are there to this day.

CAMBRIDGE

In Henry VIII's later years he had considered dissolving the University to get its lands, as he had the monasteries but, fortunately, his last wife, Katherine Parr, persuaded him against this. In fact, he ended up founding Trinity College in 1547. Elizabeth's reign saw the first of the Puritans, like Cartwright and Perkins, become famous for their preaching and learning. It was a time of roller coaster religious controversy. The Vice Chancellor and Master of Peterhouse, Dr Perne, was a good example of someone who knew how to manage the ride. Roman Catholic

under Mary and Protestant under Elizabeth, he earned from Marvell the poet the barb 'Old Andrew Turncoat', but he made light of it, despising religious passion. Fortunately, Cambridge itself was spared much actual persecution and only one protestant, the wretched John Hullier, was burnt, on Jesus Green. That religious strife was marked by burnings of Protestant or Catholic is of course obscene. Apart from theological controversy, the 16th Century was marked by social disturbances caused by price rises and enclosure. Enclosure of medieval fields

Page from facsimile of Canterbury Gospels

meant peasants losing their strips and becoming landless labourers. In 1549, Kett's Rebellion in neighbouring Norfolk provoked riots in Cambridge and fences were torn down. More peacefully, the University was given the licence to publish books and production started in 1584. This makes the Cambridge University Press the world's oldest publishing company.

IT WAS A TIME OF ROLLER COASTER RELIGIOUS CONTROVERSY

7 THE PURITANS
17th Century

CONTEXT

For many in England, the Elizabethan Church Settlement, though Protestant, was not Protestant enough. They wanted the Anglican Church to be more like the one they found in the New Testament, 'purified' of bishops and extraneous rituals. These Puritans hoped that the new Stuart dynasty from Presbyterian Scotland – James I – would be sympathetic, only to find they were deemed a threat to the religious and political order. In the reign of James I's son, Charles I, many Puritans were so discouraged that they emigrated to North America and, between 1628 and 1640, 20,000 emigrated. Those who remained were incensed by the high Church policies of Archbishop Laud and by Charles I's trying to rule without Parliament. Their religious and political anger resulted in the Civil War. This ended with the army and its great

John Bunyan

leader, Oliver Cromwell, rather than Parliament, in power. He had Charles I, 'the man of blood', executed, the House of Lords abolished and England declared a Commonwealth. Given that he had been the champion of Parliament, it was ironic that he ended up a dictator. Perhaps this was inevitable. The Civil War had unleashed radical social and economic demands like those of the Levellers and Diggers, while the Puritans became religiously divided between Presbyterians and Independents. Unpopular military rule seemed the only option. However, Puritan excesses under Cromwell, like the banning of theatre, Sunday sports and even Christmas, meant that on his death the country supported the restoration of the monarchy to Charles II. His return meant the return of the established order of squire and parson and it was the turn of the Puritans to be discriminated against as dissenters or nonconformists. Unlicensed preachers like John Bunyan found themselves in jail. However, Cromwell's struggles had not been entirely in vain. When the Catholic James II, brother and successor to Charles II, seemed to be a threat to England's Protestantism and its Parliament, the protestant William of Orange was invited from Holland in 1688 to become King and under the terms of the constitutional settlement, the Bill of Rights (the Glorious Revolution), in 1689, Parliament was to hold the real power. Of course, it was not a Parliament of the 'people', but it was to provide for greater religious and political liberty than any of the absolute monarchies in Europe. Evidence for this is found in Voltaire's *Letter Concerning the English Nation*, 1733. And in 1702 London was to see the world's first daily Newspaper, *The Daily Courant*.

COMMENT

The theology of the Puritans stressed the individual's access to God. This had huge cultural and political implications. If men could deal directly with God they could manage their own affairs, including government. They would especially oppose arbitrary royal power when it affected their consciences. Without understanding this, it is hard to explain the growth of the ideas of political liberty and constitutionalism in England and the USA. It is no coincidence that the great puritan poet John Milton (Christ's), who had been Cromwell's secretary, wrote *Areopagatica*, a major defence of the free press, the prerequisite for a free society.

CAMBRIDGE

Cambridge, home to some of the great Puritan preachers, was well disposed to the Puritans. Two colleges, Emmanuel in 1584 and Sidney Sussex in 1596, had been founded to train Puritan ministers. Emmanuel, in fact, was to provide many of the leading figures in the colonies

John Harvard

Emmanuel College

Sidney Sussex College

of New England, including John Harvard, founder of the great American University. Sidney Sussex had as one of its students the young Oliver Cromwell. During the Civil War, Cromwell was MP for Cambridge, as the town was pro-Parliament. His soldiers of the New Model Army were billeted in colleges and King's Chapel was used as a drill hall! Such insensitivities might be forgiven, but not the iconoclasm of the Puritan, William Dowsing. He destroyed many statues and stained glass windows in Cambridge, deeming them idolatrous. However, with the Restoration of the Stuarts, Puritans, like the great botanist John Ray of Trinity, were to lose their fellowships.

8 MODERN SCIENCE
17th Century

CONTEXT

While England went through the trauma of political and religious strife, an intellectual movement called the Scientific Revolution was quietly gathering momentum. Its origins went back at least to the 15th Century but it came to a head especially in the 17th Century. Essentially, it required hypothesis and experiment to understand nature. Until then 'scientific knowledge' had been based on the teaching of the Church, which relied, ironically, almost entirely on Aristotle, the pagan Greek philosopher. The impact of the Renaissance and the Reformation helped to loosen the ties of traditional authority and in 1620 Francis Bacon (Trinity) wrote his *Novum Organum Scientiarum*. He called for a study of both the 'book of God's works' – the Creation – as well as the 'book of God's word' – the Bible. In this process, traditional authorities were to be ignored and nature was to be carefully observed and investigated, with knowledge being gained by practical experiment. In Italy, Galileo was doing just this by using a telescope, confirming Copernicus's ideas of a sun-centred rather than an earth-centred universe. In a different area, William Harvey (Gonville and Caius) was showing how the circulation of the blood took place. In 1662, the Royal Society (For Improving Natural Knowledge) was founded with the Master of Trinity, John Wilkins, as the first Secretary. The person, however, who put Cambridge at the heart of this revolution was Isaac Newton. Coming to Trinity from Lincolnshire aged 19, he was at first a 'sizar', a poor student who had to work his way through college.

At 26, his brilliance made him Professor of Mathematics and in 1687 he published his great work, *Principia Mathematica*, demonstrating how gravity held our solar system together.

COMMENT

The question is sometimes raised as to why the Scientific Revolution happened in Europe. Given that it was to be the engine of modernisation, which led to the temporary pre-eminence of the West, this is no idle question. Moreover, it is made acute when we bear in mind that in the medieval period both China and the Middle East had greater scientific achievements to their credit. Why did it not then take place there? One part of the answer must surely lie in the nature of the Christian world-view. This presupposed a God who made men with reason and therefore that his Creation was orderly and reasonable. It was going to have natural laws capable of comprehension. This God had also mandated that mankind should have dominion over nature. Therefore, science and technology were not only possible but right and proper. In his book *The Grand Titration*, 1969, Joseph Needham (Gonville and Caius), the great authority on Chinese science and technology, explains why China did not progress scientifically as might have been expected: 'There was no confidence that the code of Nature's Laws could ever be unveiled, because there was no assurance that a divine being even more rational than ourselves, had ever formulated such a code capable of being read.' Some may argue that the Church obstructed science, as in the case of Galileo's being forced to recant, but that was the Church holding to Aristotle, not the Bible, and this was recognised. In fact, most scientists at this time were deeply religious. Newton held that 'God is the God of order and not confusion' and 'I shall make no discovery unless it is imparted by the Holy Spirit'.

CAMBRIDGE

Cambridge had a reputation for being unhealthy and liable to plague and fever. In fact, Isaac Newton conceived some of his key work while at home during an outbreak of plague in the town. Part of the problem was the King's Ditch. Originally dug as a defence for the city in the 10th Century, it was used later as a rubbish dump and site for latrines. Another was the absence of a clean water supply. In 1610, the town, under the wealthy hostelry owner, Thomas Hobson, built Hobson's Conduit, which still runs, though no longer as the water supply. In 1615, Dr Perse (Gonville and Caius) founded the Free School which still bears his name, a notable school but no longer free. The original school building now houses the University Whipple Museum of the History of Science, well worth a visit. Later in the century, Cambridge benefited from a family connection. Matthew Wren, Master of Pembroke and an

Hobson's Conduit

ardent royalist, had been imprisoned in the Tower under Cromwell. There he made an oath that if released alive he would build a new chapel for his college. When this happened, he

Wren Library, Trinity College

got in touch with his young nephew, Christopher, a talented mathematician from Oxford with an interest in architecture. The young man went on to build not just Pembroke Chapel but also Emmanuel Chapel and the exquisite Wren Library at Trinity all in the new neoclassical style. A useful contact indeed.

Pembroke College Chapel

9 THE AGE OF REASON
18th Century

CONTEXT

The religious strife of the 17th Century in this country and Europe led to a desire for toleration, as argued by John Locke in his *Essay On Toleration*, 1689. People began to look to 'impartial' human reason rather than fractious divine revelation as the arbiter of truth. Philosophy replaced theology and sceptical inquiry took the place of biblical debate. It is called the Age of Reason or the Enlightenment. Locke and Hume in this country paralleled the philosophers of Europe, such as Voltaire and Kant. The Church reflected this cultural shift and became 'broad' or latitudinarian. It was too

Wimpole Hall

often a time of religious torpor with the parson as likely to be fox-hunting as preparing a sermon or visiting the sick. The great aristocrats and landed gentry, with their neo-classical houses like Wimpole Hall just outside Cambridge, ruled unchallenged through an increasingly corrupt Parliament.

Into this vacuum of spiritual and social decay came a major religious revival. In this country it was associated with the itinerant open-air preaching of John Wesley and George Whitefield. Out of it came the Methodists and the revived Anglican evangelicals who turned their attention to social reform like the abolition of slavery and missionary endeavour. The reaction of others to the enervating rule of reason and encroaching ugliness of the Industrial Revolution was a passionate celebration of human feeling centring on the beauties of nature. This was coupled with, at least in youth, a political radicalism inspired by the French Revolution, 1789. Poets were the typical spokesmen of this Romantic Movement and Cambridge saw Coleridge (Jesus), Wordsworth (St John's) and Byron (Trinity) all pass through. Byron, who as a student was fond of boxing and kept a bear, had this to say of his tutor, 'Unlucky Tavell, doomed to daily cares by pugilistic pupils and by bears'.

COMMENT

REASON

The 18th Century Age of Reason or Enlightenment was the crucial watershed in Europe's becoming both secular and modern. Hume in Scotland and Kant in Prussia seemed to have destroyed the traditional proofs for the existence of God, while the ideals of liberty, equality and fraternity seemed self-evidently adequate. But already with Hume the reliance on reason had led to a radical scepticism. All truth was now undermined, but this was overlooked. Also, the failure of the French Revolution to live by its ideals caused for most only a distaste for extremism, rather than a real questioning of human moral self-sufficiency.

RELIGION (EVANGELICALS)

In Cambridge, the religious revival was associated with the career of Charles Simeon, 1759-1836, Fellow of Kings and vicar of Holy Trinity for 54 years. Bitterly opposed by his parishioners at the beginning of his work, his preaching and pastoral care, including great generosity during a local famine, won him enormous respect. He was a mentor to many young ministers and was involved in the start of the Church Missionary Society in 1799. His rooms were in the Gibbs building in King's College upon whose roof he was accustomed to go for early morning prayer. Of the same generation was William Wilberforce 1759-1833 whose career was one of the great fruits of the religious revival, though not initially. As a wealthy young man about town, Wilberforce was more likely to be found drinking at The Eagle than studying at St John's. Only his conversion, and advice from John Newton, the ex-slaver and author of

The Eagle public house

'Amazing Grace', set him on his path. This led to the abolition of the slave trade in 1807 and, finally, of slavery itself in the British Empire in 1833. Interestingly, he understood his Christian vocation to be in politics, 'My walk, I am sensible, is a public one. My business is in the world'. This was true for his circle of friends in the Clapham Sect who were to be influential in social reform.

CAMBRIDGE

Increasing wealth meant improvements for Cambridge. The town centre, starting with Petty Cury, was lit and paved. Banks, theatres and coaching inns were built and Capability Brown landscaped the backs of St John's. In 1744, *The Cambridge Journal* became the town's first newspaper while the shop Eaden Lilley opened towards the end of the century. In 1776, Addenbrooke's Hospital was founded on the proceeds of a will from a local physician. The Senate House, built in 1730, replaced Great St Mary's, which had been in use since

The Senate House

medieval times, as the place where students were given their degrees – though note that at this time noblemen could still get a degree without taking an exam! Since the end of the medieval and feudal period, students were no longer poor clerks but increasingly the sons of the gentry and nobility for whom the University was a kind of finishing school. College architecture reflected this by becoming rather grand. Downing College, for example, founded in 1800, looks like a great country house. Academic standards were generally low. In 1807 Byron wrote in a letter, 'the place is wretched enough – a villainous chaos of din and drunkenness, nothing but hazard and burgundy, hunting, mathematics and Newmarket, rot and racing. Yet it is paradise.' Enough said.

10 THE VICTORIANS
19th Century

CONTEXT

The Victorian era under the engine of the Industrial Revolution was a period of unparalleled change. Steam power, factories, railways, teeming cities with fashionable squares and wretched slums all came into view. In the century after the first census in 1801 the population rocketed from 14 to 40 million. Victorian society was young and energetic. It saw a mixture of laissez-faire indifference and high-minded reform that just avoided revolution. It enlarged the electorate, trimmed the worst abuses in economic and political life and mostly avoided European war in favour of imperial acquisition. After the shock of the French Revolution and under the influence of the religious revival it was a respectable churchgoing society. There was hypocrisy, but there was also charity and reform. Lord Shaftesbury, with his Factory Acts, and William Booth, with his Salvation Army, were amongst the most notable. Their efforts meant that Karl Marx, grinding his teeth in the British Museum, producing Das Kapital, 1867, was listened to more in Europe than in Britain. Nonetheless, Christianity can only claim to have ameliorated some of the excesses of the Industrial Revolution in all its harshness and exploitation.

**VICTORIAN SOCIETY
WAS YOUNG
AND ENERGETIC**

COMMENT

DOUBT

If most Victorians still went to Church or Chapel, the cultural elite were bedevilled by the onset of increasing religious doubt. Matthew Arnold lamented this ebbing of the sea of faith, 'its melancholy, long, withdrawing roar', in his poem Dover Beach, 1867. Charles Lyell's *Principles of Geology*, 1836, doubted a six day creation, David Strauss's *Life of Jesus*, 1836, translated by George Eliot, depicted the gospels as myth and Darwin's *Origin of Species*, 1859, seemed to provide a satisfactory alternative to divine creation. A secular temper was in formation. Marx's ideas of religion as the opium of the people and Freud's ideas that religion was a neurosis merely fuelled the disenchantment. But not all conceded to it. Famous scientists like Michael Faraday and Clerk Maxwell, first head of the Cavendish Laboratory, remained staunch believers, while the Cambridge biblical scholars, Lightfoot, Hort and Westcott did much to shore up the credibility of the Bible.

MISSION

One of the ironies of the 19th Century was that while doubt gained ground at home, missionary endeavour abroad was spreading Christianity far and wide. In 1857, Livingstone came to the Senate House to rouse a concern for Africa and was so enthusiastically received that it led to the start of the University Mission to Central Africa. Later, the Cambridge Seven, a privileged group of Cambridge undergraduates, including the England cricketer C. T. Studd, drew widespread comment when they volunteered for the China Inland Mission.

CAMBRIDGE

THE TOWN

The 1835 Municipal Corporation Act helped to reform the town which the Parliamentary Commission had found particularly corrupt and some progress became possible. But it was not until 1856 that the town's subordination to the University and its symbol, the Black Assembly, was abolished. This explains why, when the railways came in 1845, the University had been able to insist that the station for the noisy, smelly trains which might also lure students to London was put far from the town centre. The railway was to kill the coach and river trade, but became an important new employer and led to the eastern expansion of the town. Chivers, making jam with local fruit, was another big

The Pumping Station

employer, while in 1876 William Heffer started his bookshop. In 1895, the pumping station, now a museum, with its deep sewers ended the practice of putting raw sewage into the river and made the river more pleasant for recreation.

THE UNIVERSITY

The Victorians were altogether more serious than their 18th Century forbears. Religious revival and the challenges of the Industrial Revolution and Empire made sure of that. Prince Albert, who became Chancellor of the University in 1847, represented this serious and progressive impulse. He was particularly concerned for scientific education and in 1874 the Cavendish Laboratory was opened with Clerk Maxwell as its first Director. Other reforms followed. The religious tests that had stopped non-Anglicans having University posts were abolished in 1871. Women's colleges were founded – Girton in 1869 and Newnham in 1871 (though women could not obtain degrees until 1948) and dons were allowed to marry from 1882. Students started to work harder for a wider variety of subjects like Science, Engineering and Modern Languages. They also played harder, as organised games like cricket, football and rugby, as well as rowing, became avenues to glory. In 1825, the Cricket Club was formed and in 1829 the first Boat Race against Oxford took place. Not all the Victorians were sporting philistines; in 1815 the Union Society for Debate was started, as was the Cambridge University Musical Society in 1843 and in 1851 the Amateur Dramatic Club – all still thriving. The relocation of the Botanic Gardens and the foundation of the Fitzwilliam Museum also increased the range of tastes and pleasures.

The Fitzwilliam Museum

11 THE TWENTIETH CENTURY

CONTEXT

What can be said? Many of you remember it. It was an age of conflict made terrible by science. There were the two major world wars, caused by national rivalries, which led to the eclipse of Europe and a major revolution in Russia, inspired by social hatred, which was later to lead to the Cold War. Amidst it all was the incomprehensible horror of the Holocaust. Meanwhile, Western high culture in its art, music and literature was imploding, bereft of meaning or hope. In the 'Third World', scores of other smaller wars and revolutions were interspersed with natural disasters. Like the 19th Century, it was a time of relentless change on all fronts. Nuclear weapons recast international relations, the contraceptive pill recast the family, the computer recast work and television recast culture. The world itself was becoming a global village, inescapably interdependent.

COMMENT

When Europe abandoned Christianity as credulous and backward what did it replace it with? The darkness of Nazism and Communism. Was it not cultures like the USA that retained their Christian foundations that preserved liberal democracy? And did not those same Christian values help in the recovery of post-war western Europe and in the undermining of Communism in eastern Europe?

THE SECULAR FUTURE?

The collapse of Communism in the late 20th Century led some to speak of the triumph of capitalist democracy and the 'end of history' and others to warn of the 'clash of civilisations'. Whatever the outcome, is the West or the world equipped to face the future? In the West at least, the dominant cultural leitmotif is no longer Christianity, no longer even 'modernist' humanism (though some still think so) but 'postmodernist' relativism. This is the conviction that there is no ultimate truth or morality, that there is no overarching intellectual framework and that no culture has more to offer than any other. Is this not the mantra of the blind leading the blind? How will we judge and contain the inevitable new technologies and shape a humane society? Can the Christian Gospel of personal salvation and cultural redemption, with many centuries achievement to its credit, be so lightly cast aside? Some will argue that science has made religion obsolete. But it was Einstein who said, 'a legitimate conflict between science and religion cannot exist'. Perhaps too often science

is invoked to justify materialist assumptions pure and simple, i.e. that 'matter' or 'nature' is all that there is, and that of course is a philosophical perspective rather than a strictly scientific one. Moreover, it reduces us all to things, with no meaning or value. C. S. Lewis, the writer and Christian apologist, who was Professor of English here in his later years, well describes the consequences of this outlook in his novel, *That Hideous Strength*.

CAMBRIDGE

The terrible losses of the First World War were shared by town and gown alike, as the war memorials in the town and college chapels testify. The social distress common in the 19th Cen-

The American Cemetery, Cambridge

tury continued until the foundation of the welfare state. In 1904, 1 in 3 families was below the poverty line and 1 in 8 babies died in its first year. In the 1926 General Strike 2,000 undergraduates 'played' strike breaker. Philby, Blunt and Burgess, the cold war spies and traitors, were all students in the '30s. Their foolish Communism was partly a reaction against the conjunction of privilege and poverty. In the Second World War, Cambridge was fortunate to escape the brunt of the bombing.

Any damage was confined to near the railway which, thanks to the prejudice of the 19th Century dons, was far from the town centre. However, around Cambridge were the great airfields essential to the war effort. Losses in the air were heavy, as can be seen at the American Cemetery just to the west of the town. The war was nonetheless a motor for social change and university grants for students in 1944 broadened access. It was in science that, in the 20th Century, Cambridge achieved particular distinction. Before the war, Rutherford split the atom and after it Crick and Watson unravelled DNA. These were only the most notable of many discoveries. This success in science, along with some home-grown industry like engineering at Marshalls, has enabled Cambridge to become a major centre of the UK's high-tech economy – the 'Fenomenon'. Microsoft, the NAPP Laboratories, the Human Genome Project and the National Plant Breeding Institute are just some of the names and the Trinity Business Park and St John's Innovation Centre just two of the sites. Along with the 4 million tourists a year, they help to maintain the city's prosperity in the 21st Century.

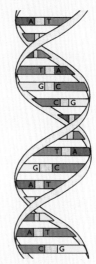

The Schlumberger Building

α I AM WHO I AM Ω

12 KEY CHRISTIAN TEXTS

THE CREATION MANDATE

Genesis 1:26,27

Then God said, "Let us make man in our image, in our likeness, and let them rule over the fish of the sea and the birds of the air, over the livestock, over all the earth, and over all the creatures that move along the ground." So God created man in his own image, in the image of God he created him; male and female he created them.

THE FALL

Genesis 3:1-5

Now the serpent was more crafty than any of the wild animals the LORD had made. He said to the woman, "Did God really say, 'You must not eat from any tree in the garden'?" The woman said to the serpent, "We may eat fruit from the trees in the garden, but God did say, 'You must not eat fruit from the tree that is in the middle of the garden, and you must not touch it, or you will die.'" "You will surely not die," the serpent said to the woman. "For God knows that when you eat of it your eyes will be opened, and you will be like God, knowing good and evil."

THE WRATH OF GOD

Romans 1:18-20

The wrath of God is being revealed from heaven against all the godlessness and wickedness of men who suppress the truth by their wickedness, since what may be known about God is plain to them, because God has made it plain to them. For since the creation of the world God's invisible qualities – his eternal power and divine nature – have been clearly seen, being understood from what has been made, so that men are without excuse.

THE LOVE OF GOD

John 3:16

For God so loved the world that he gave his one and only Son, that whoever believes in him should not perish but have eternal life.

A NEW HEAVEN AND A NEW EARTH

Revelation 21:1-4

Then I saw a new heaven and a new earth, for the first heaven and the first earth had passed away, and there was no longer any sea. I saw the Holy City, the new Jerusalem, coming down out of heaven from God, prepared as a bride beautifully dressed for her husband. And I heard a loud voice from the throne saying, "Now the dwelling of God is with men, and he will live with them. They will be his people, and God himself will be with them and be their God. He will wipe every tear from their eyes. There will be no more death or mourning or crying or pain, for the old order of things has passed away".

THE TEN COMMANDMENTS

Exodus 20:1-17

And God spoke all these words:
"I am the LORD your God, who brought you out of Egypt, out of the land of slavery.
"You shall have no other gods before me.

"You shall not make for yourself an idol in the form of anything in heaven above or on the earth beneath or in the waters below.

"You shall not misuse the name of the LORD your God, for the LORD will not hold anyone guiltless who misuses his name.

"Remember the Sabbath day by keeping it holy. Six days you shall labour and do all your work, but the seventh day is a Sabbath to the LORD your God…

"Honour your father and your mother, so that you may live long in the land the LORD your God is giving you.

"You shall not murder.

"You shall not commit adultery.

"You shall not steal.

"You shall not give false testimony against your neighbour.

"You shall not covet your neighbour's house. You shall not covet your neighbour's wife, or his manservant or maidservant, his ox or donkey, or anything that belongs to your neighbour."

THE BEATITUDES

Matthew 5:3-12

Blessed are the poor in spirit, for theirs is the kingdom of heaven. Blessed are those who mourn, for they will be comforted. Blessed are the meek, for they will inherit the earth. Blessed are those who hunger and thirst for righteousness, for they will be filled. Blessed are the merciful, for they will be shown mercy. Blessed are the pure in heart, for they will see God. Blessed are the peacemakers, for they will be called sons of God. Blessed are those who are persecuted because of righteousness, for theirs is the kingdom of heaven. Blessed are you when people insult you, persecute you and falsely say all kinds of evil against you because of me. Rejoice and be glad, because great is your reward in heaven, for in the same way they persecuted the prophets who were before you.

LOVE

1 Corinthians 13:4-8a

Love is patient, love is kind. It does not envy, it does not boast, it is not proud. It is not rude, it is not self-seeking, it is not easily angered, it keeps no record of wrongs. Love does not delight in evil but rejoices with the truth. It always protects, always trusts, always hopes, always perseveres. Love never fails.

THE LORD'S PRAYER

Book of Common Prayer based on Matthew 6

Our Father which art in heaven,
Hallowed be thy Name,
Thy kingdom come,
Thy will be done, in earth as it is in heaven.
Give us this day our daily bread;
And forgive us our trespasses, As we forgive them that trespass against us;
And lead us not into temptation, but deliver us from evil.
For thine is the kingdom, the power, and the glory,
For ever and ever. Amen

THE APOSTLES' CREED

Book of Common Prayer

I believe in God the Father Almighty, Maker of heaven and earth;
And in Jesus Christ his only Son our Lord, Who was conceived by the Holy Ghost, Born of the Virgin Mary, Suffered under Pontius Pilate, Was crucified, dead, and buried: He descended into hell; The third day he rose again from the dead; He ascended into heaven, And sitteth on the right hand of God the Father Almighty; From thence he shall come to judge the quick and the dead.
I believe in the Holy Ghost; The holy Catholic Church; The Communion of Saints;
The Forgiveness of sins; The Resurrection of the body, And the life everlasting.

Bible quotations from the New International Version

CHRISTIAN
HERITAGE
CAMBRIDGE

Many of the things we take for granted in our present secular culture, such as universities, scientific discovery, constitutional government and our ideas of human rights, were actually made possible by the Christian foundations of our culture in the past. They didn't come out of nowhere, but from a particular matrix of ideas and values. Christian Heritage sets out to remind people of this by its work as a visitor centre in the Round Church. Here is the exhibition on which this booklet is based, as well as the DVD *Saints and Scholars*. The church is also the base for our guided walks around the city and university. As people will probably be aware, our past Christian culture wasn't always consistent in its practice and therefore there is an irony in the fact that we are situated in a building, The Round Church, which was built, originally in the 12th Century, trying to promote Crusades! However, having acknowledged that, we do want to draw attention to the good things that Christianity has done. In addition to the work of the visitor centre, Christian Heritage engages with the present, by being the base for lectures, summer schools and a student training programme. It remains a place of active Christian witness in our secular culture and all are most welcome.

Production of this booklet
kindly sponsored by

David Ball
Group Ltd

www.davidballgroup.com

"Concrete innovation is our passion"

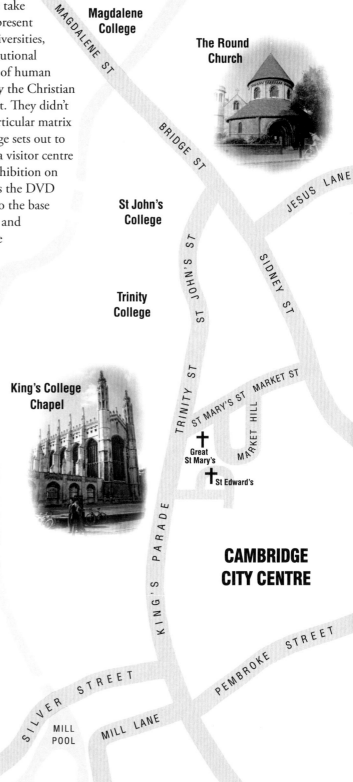

Magdalene College

The Round Church

St John's College

Trinity College

King's College Chapel

Great St Mary's

St Edward's

CAMBRIDGE CITY CENTRE

MAGDALENE ST
BRIDGE ST
JESUS LANE
ST JOHN'S ST
SIDNEY ST
TRINITY ST
ST MARY'S ST
MARKET ST
MARKET HILL
KING'S PARADE
RIVER CAM
PEMBROKE STREET
SILVER STREET
MILL POOL
MILL LANE